*IN THIS KINGDOM
BY THE SEA*

IN THIS KINGDOM
BY THE SEA

POEMS BY
W. G. McNEICE

*Set in Ballardvale type and printed in the Republic of Ireland
by The Kerryman Ltd.*

THE KERRYMAN LTD.
*Clash Industrial Estate, Tralee,
Co. Kerry, Ireland.*

First Irish edition, 1983

BRITISH LIBRARY CATALOGUING IN PUBLICATION DATA

W. G. McNeice

IN THIS KINGDOM BY THE SEA

ISBN 946277 06 0 H/bk

She was a child and I was a child,
In this kingdom by the sea.

(Edgar Allan Poe)

To Mary

ACKNOWLEDGEMENTS

Many of these poems first appeared in: *The Irish Times, Irish Independent, The Irish Press* (New Irish Writing), *The Dubliner, Poetry Ireland, The Times Literary Supplement, Irish Poets 1924–74, Poetry Ireland Review, Shannonside* and *The Kerryman.*

CONTENTS

KILSHANNIG

A dark-haired girl feeds
calves under the August sky; the sea
cascades on the path that leads
to a cemetery where crosses, knee-
deep in grass, grace the horizon, seed
in vain. Spaniards lie
here like quicken in forests that bred
armadas, and nearby
a few houses cluster, encased
in silence. Each year
we come for dilisk picked after high tide
on the islands, tasting
of time and tides mated in fear,
of memories mostly in hiding.

RITUAL

Glow of gorse fires on the skyline,
the air abrasive with the tang –
no Paschal blaze to undermine
immemorial gods with a bang

of thaumaturgic fire – but a fine
inferno of furze, sharpening
the hills where sheep hang
like snowdrops in the spring.

IN MEMORY OF PATRICK KAVANAGH

Paths become accustomed to the feel
of feet, fields to the incisive plough,
birds to man. Gull and starling reel
over the headland where the raw earth-sow
turns on her belly – all in a day's work.
But in the mind unquiet thoughts still lurk.

He wrote of frost and the stiffness of grass,
of silence, that is God-made, of the sound
of shifting feet at the ritual of mass,
of lonely men who borrow from the ground
long winter nights, their skin hardened by sun –
and hands that tell the time by thirty-one.

They will recall him now in Monaghan,
at Iniskeen, beyond which darkened fields
melt into emptiness – the poet-man
who swopped it for the soul a city shields
behind closed doors, and found a solitude
in numbers – words, words – but little food.

All in a day's work, a life's pause.
He is back by familiar roads that dissipate
in distance, by fields burnished by winter haws
where the world is hinged to a rusty farmyard gate.
They have survived him, even survive his words.
Some shall remember how he once crossed swords.

NO PHOENIX

No one heard
her crying in the white
silence of snow. Flames fired
the thatch and the red light
became rose-hued,
hissing in rivers of water
that spurted like blood.
She cried: my daughter –
asleep in her room!
No one was near
to hold her as she slumped; fumes
burned at her nostrils, fear
in her breast:
glass splintered and broke
as the house collapsed in a holocaust
of acrid smoke.

No one heard
her crying in the white
graveyard of snow. Weird
crosses obstructed the light
of dawn where charred
wood and walls blackened and burned
stood out. And the snared
child was interned
forever in that bleak scene,
indistinguishable now
from the obscene
rubble and surrounding snow.

A new house may supplant
the old; a new spring
discover the earth – but nothing can
make of the child a maturer thing.

BEYOND THESE ISLANDS

The sea begins where seeing ends,
beyond these islands where men say
totalitarian time descends.

Here I remember certain friends,
one who is dead, for whom I pray
the sea begins where seeing ends.

He loved it dark when evening sends
the curlew crying and the way
totalitarian time descends

where all-but-bleeding fuchsia bends
before the brute wind's disarray.
The sea begins where seeing ends

and an Atlantic void defends
his memory, where day by day
totalitarian time descends

on every island that contends
with elemental interplay.
The sea begins, where seeing ends
totalitarian time descends.

WINTER PARALLEL

1

I come on a world that has been
before and will again,
familiar world of winter that to men
begins with death. The grass keeps green
though with a ghosted grey
of frost still fresh from yesterday
held in the hollow of a blade
that was in summer made.

2

In cold of day's last glow
I see a house that speechless stands
upon its own bed-ridden lands;
there half a century ago
it faced the west with brazen stare
and challenged stupidly the air,
the wildest element,
to blow it down. . . .
Walls that were white are brown,
and cracked and broken the cement.

3

Quiet fields attract the gloom
and trees are naked now,
there's not a leaf on any bough
and silence seems to echo doom.
Bushes like sticks to pick the eye
sign-post the villain sky.
Suddenly comes a bark of sound –
a dead leaf crackles across the ground –
the wind descends to lay the dead
deep in its dark and final bed.

4

The shadow of a chimney pot
flashes over the roof
as starlight from a world aloof,
will-o'-the-wisp of light is caught
sneaking into a room;
a faint perfume
pervades, like liquid drops of memory,
what senses feel or see –
then all at once the seasons fly
time to deceive the eye,
with sound and silence of forgotten days,
of childhood loves and childhood ways,
a young boy's dream
suddenly surfacing like cream –
through these great parishes of past,
secure in love,
does my child-spirit rove
freely at last?

5

The night has fallen on a world of shape
and swallowed it like Jonah's whale;
nature succumbs to winter's flail
knowing of no escape.
One state endures while others die
beneath the everlasting sky;
a dread destroying power has set
upon the minions of the spring –
summer is gone and autumn a past thing –
winter is hand in glove with death!

6

Now that I have gone by
this house, outdistanced memory,
in midnight black when I no longer see
the stars that sowed the sky
with brilliant light,
I, too, am swallowed by the night,
and all the past that instantaneous thought
had resurrected in that timeless spot,
leaving a world of winter in its place
no consolations can efface.

AUTUMN ARABESQUE

A hood of twilight caught the sky
and hawk-like the world became
quiet, feeding the passer-by
with a flow of thought from the same
spring of shadow, night,
where death walks in delight
with the passer-by (like Christ
unrecognised on the road to Emmaus) –
the darkness streaming from his poised
imponderable jaws.

ASPECTS OF LIGHT

1

I often polished the linoleum
for my mother on a morning
when the dust in the room
stood up like a pillar

in the sunlight. I applied
the wax polish with vigour,
absorbing the scent on the side.
The pleasure was in the shining,

and the sunlight glossed
the surface with approval –
the displaced dust
hung homeless in a cloud.

My heart hankered after the light
outside like a seed in a pod.

2

Drawing back the curtains on the wide
window in the bedroom was like
the creation of light as the tide
of the sun flooded the room

with the shock of a nuclear flash.
I had to turn away to adjust my eyes
to the revelation. June was a-thresh
in the out-of-doors with the spittle of sound

in the ears – I could hear the birds,
vital with song, in the elder trees,
and the constant click of insect swords
in the grass. You were pretending to sleep,

your face averted from the light,
your hair resplendent in a golden heap.

3

Returning home on Christmas Eve
by car, tired eyes kept wide
by wonder, the sky was a sieve
of stars shimmering.

pigeon-holed in space. Frost
metalled the road with diamonds
of grit, and in the furthermost
houses, vaguely discernible

across dark ditch and field,
candles twitched like glow-worms
in windows and annealed
the Nativity in stained glass –

Jesus with Joseph and Mary,
the stable, the ox and the ass.

AND NOT A MOMENT TOO SOON

And not a moment too soon
the cherry trees break into bloom,
fragile, pink-pale-petalled stars
swaying unsteadily in the air –
yet they have April written there
perfect in each pink-petalled stare,
where soon (too soon for me)
there will not be a bloom on a cherry tree.

EVENING, FAHAMORE

Seagulls share their open-air delight
acrobating high above the pier,
mirrored on water delicately bright;
down by the slipway yet another year
has verdigrised the cut stone with a ring
of sudden age, impassively endured.
Across the water like a vagrant thing
a beetled curragh, rhythmically oared,
measures the loneliness of vacant seas
against the skyline where dispersing light
patterns the level sands of Maharees
with pencil-dark declivities of night.

THE SEA

The sea emotionally drags a hand
across the wind-indented sand –
plover or curlew, which one of you cries?
you are near to my heart as love that lies
silent and unsought. Shall it waste away
as your night sounds in the round of day?

The silence is in the sea, ignored
and familiar; in it is stored
the resentment in me for I know
every stone of its shingle, every blow
on its agonised body. We are bound
together by each other's wound.

What do they know of the merciless sea
who come to its anonymity
with words out of Synge or Sayers – a dream
of the poet's imagination, theme
for a book or a play? I know it well
as whorled and impounded shell.

Tomas and Paud have gone to join
Micheal and Sean. It is a sign
of the times. There is more to be gleaned in
                              New York
from unskilled and uncomplimentary work.
But God has designated me
grass-widow to the mulish sea.

MONT SAINTE-VICTOIRE

The sun is high, his eyes are bleeding –
brightness clinical, shadow – sharp, defined,
light and dark clear-cut as diamond,
air hot with the mistral wind,
water warm as wine from Provence;
distance a reflection of colours combined,
shape an obstacle in the path of light;
detail acknowledged, discarded like the rind
of an orange – all he can see is the mountain.

All he could ever see was the mountain, dark
and dominating, huge in the local sky,
as if God dwelt in its windy storeys. Clerk
in his father's bank, he had tried as a youth
to ascend it, had failed short of the summit.
Painted it a hundred times since –
from all aspects – but could never plumb its
secret, its fascination for him, that bogged
                              him down
eternally in Aix, an outcast in the town.

CHILDREN OF LIR

Where placid waters hide
all that is beautiful,
ephemeral, they glide
with such indifference
of grace that only a fool
would count sordid pence
and not these twenty swans
at Fenit sheltering,
that drift into the bronze
age of evening light,
each migratory wing
anchored against the night.

JACK

Dublin could not tame your tongue
nor your midland eye for space;
all those years sheltering among
grey houses greyed your face.
The tools of trade, the love of wood
your father gave you, laid aside
now; the watering of the blood
begun – the art of the crucified.

In Delvin wild ducks break
wings over the whiskered lake;
a boat lies idle there; cows
circumnavigate the house.
Looking down on fields and streams
where the Boyne drainage now redeems
rich pastureland, you must have known
the bitterness of bog and stone.

"The house that Jack built" on this site,
extended knows the inner joy
of children growing there by right;
the second generation fly
the city to revitalise
the dormant and neglected land
that once you measured with the eyes
as one would measure time with sand.

In Delvin country people rise
to catch the wild duck by surprise.
Salmon in the Inny spawn,
the sparkle in their movement gone,
while blackbirds from the Crooked Wood
evaluate the neighbourhood.
But you have left it to begin
another day with other kin.

MEMORIES

Corralled off-shore white horses leap
and foam on warm encircled sands;
at bleak Kilshannig old men sleep
where half a ruined church wall stands.
You brought us there that April day
when winds blew blind uncertain holes
in multiplying sea-horse spray
and ruffled unassuming shoals.

Among the gravestones, one, you said,
designed by you "commemorates
the hermit monks of Brandon Head;
a cross with slanted arms restates
the ancient heritage of faith".
The ocean in the distance ran
on island bridgeheads, now in spate,
beyond where shielded eyes could scan.

FOR THE FEAST OF ST. MARY MAGDALEN

Which man of us has not dreamed Christ at his side
in the lonely dark, prominent with light, serene;
only to find that momentary pride
whipped by a whirlwind and another scene
backdropped in place when the market disarray
of day dawned and Christ's compassionate face
mooned into vacant silence, lowered away,
and the strong were made weak and the weak were
                                        in disgrace?

But you, Magdalen, dried his feet with your hair,
emptied your heart of evil, made it full
as the moon's involvement; and those who once
                                        watched you rake
the city streets were now taken unaware
by one who had strangely become more beautiful
than Sheba – who had sorrowed for his sake.

FAYA LARGEAU

1

Morning-anointed, long shadows leap
from the source of light
in the vaporous distance where date-palms
begin in uncertain height
and spectral figures merge in white.

Dark and anonymous two women walk
barefoot on the sand,
balancing baskets on their heads;
one has a child in hand
half-hidden like contraband.

2

Now in silence, pin-drop still,
this image-clad
reflection of a quiet oasis
in forgotten Chad,
lingers like a hesitant nomad.

NOW IN MARCH

Familiar as a goat track
this road to Dingle town,
twisting like a corkscrew
into the sky. Now in March
the blue dazzle of snow
on mountains and the dry down
drifted to tangled heather
camouflages sheep to look
as if the snow had feet
and moved mountains to Mahomet.

Up, up, into the sun
beyond the river of shadows,
until the sea rings round
and boats puff inward
gliding still as swans.
We miss the fuchsia hedges'
crimson and the heather's gold;
but then, their crop will glow
with incandescent fire
summer and autumn soon.

Returning later the sky
is sure-fire with snow showers,
changeable as a chameleon
and intermittent with sun-blue
on Brandon, distantly cold
as a Swiss canton postcard –
through Gleann na nGealt
where the sea breaks white
on reaches of golden sand
as far as the eye can see.

GIRALDUS CAMBRENSIS

Giraldus, man of the woods,
as tutor to Prince John
on a moonlighting trip to Ireland
when the rebels were overrun,

compiled his topography
in the classic mould
of French and Latin scholars
from what he saw and was told.

Not all he heard was fact
nor all he wrote untrue
concerning the peasant Irish,
but an amalgam of the two,
that pleased the Oxford clerics,
the Welsh one, too.

A TOUCH OF FROST

The frost had argued all the night
until the grass was tongue-tied white;

red roofs that shimmered in the sun
last evening soon expired as one,

caught in the sky's intensive frown
where china-blue stars settled down
like hatching hens above the town.

Morning brought birds to their knees,
the silence filled with passive pleas,

and water pooled unstoppered light
in icy rainbows for delight:

my mountains wore an ermine cloak
when furtive chimneys dribbled smoke
and insulated humans woke.

ALL THAT SHE HAD

Wearily her eyes closed
for the last time. Her face
had wrinkles like snow-
drifts in a sheltered place.

She gave to the world
time and energy –
all that she had. Now gnarled
she lies like a felled tree.

No one can deny
that the greatness men write
about here lies
accomplished tonight.

ISLAND DAWN

Moonlight pearls through stunted trees,
silver-washes Blasket walls;
beneath us, dark dissembling seas
break in endless caterwauls.

Breathless we hurry down the path,
stumbling over stones and roots,
as dawn's intensive aftermath
censors the owl's objecting hoots.

Returning when his boat had gone,
the sky an almost chalk-white mass
the sun had opened to the bone,
I break the dew-seal of the grass.

NOT TO BYZANTIUM BUT ROME

Not to Byzantium but Rome sailing
with the wind steady before and behind,
the tern and noisy kittiwake reeling
above me – all the images I find
in a barren frame of mind.

Birds are beauty of blood in motion
not hammered images of gold
impaled beyond tormented oceans,
stifled in dreams, cast in a mould
of erotic movement – dusty, old.

Time does not recede. The passing
years move to fulfilment not decay;
there is no art without compassion,
and once the model has dreamed away
Knossos and Mycenae are clay.

Beauty is part of the animate
kingdom that has cast off the dead,
and the noblest of all is creative man,
whom God made, for whom Christ died,
being worthy of this as sages said.

May no unfriendly storm dismantle
my sail, distract me, misdirect,
shipwreck (as once to Paul on Malta)
as even men of intellect
founder and fall, divide, dissect.

Peter is port – and to this symbol
city sailing I leave behind
the land of distant gong and cymbal,
tacked to a fresh and healthy wind
to blow the cobwebs from the mind.

THE STARLING HEART

In crushed silence of October
the starlings linger by the chimney pot,
costumed for panic, sober
as circus clowns in their mottled
indifference to the season's mood.
You, too, of the starling heart,
are no stranger to fortitude,
no glasscase princess apart
from the world, but immersed in the strain –
loyal, loving, and tempered by time
to grow strong in the recess of pain
like a rose that frost cannot tame.

SONG

Fingers of twilight
darken and thicken
like berries on branches
of beautiful quicken.

Daylight is greying
ember by ember;
the hands of the clock
are in league with November.

O draw down the curtain
on dying October,
the cry of the curlew
is mournfully sober,

and time's superstition
runs darkly for cover,
for this is the night
when the dead pass over.

THE PEACE OF THE WATER

Like black ice the Boyne dissembles
the dark sky of June,
sultry and petulant. The water
prides like a lion
with strong claws cleaving
the wooded countryside,
the rich unmutilated
pastureland once denied
to us by red-bellied planters
who grew soft on the potion
of game and leisurely hunting,
pomade and lotion.

God grant us freedom from their likes,
even our countrymen;
grant us the peace of the water
to reflect on the waterhen
quietly minding her business
in a ribbon of reeds
by the strong brew of the river,
finding enough for her needs
and not accumulating hate
by greed where once cannon
and musket smoke clouded forever
divergent opinion.

Grant us the peace of the water,
communion of streams
blending uniquely together,
whose confluence redeems
bog water and springs from the hilltops
mingled and powerfully deep
spinning by Slane where Laoghaire
and the king's three daughters sleep,

undisturbed by frenetic imposters,
under the sky's gold coin
in midsummer beauty
by the unpragmatic Boyne.

FOR MY FATHER

In Delvin I became my father,
saw through his eyes the old house brighten
early each day, the dark bog water
mirror the wild duck's deft maneouvres,
and the waterhen dart like the tongue of a python
into the rushes, turf placed to dry
by the lake's edge and the opulent sky
that the sun with an orient eye discovers.

In Delvin I became my father;
day-dreamt in fields where cattle hung
their heavy heads among strong fodder,
and where cold winds of winter yelled
on yellow grass – and in among
grey, decimated trees I found
traces of children all around
and knew that his were there as well.

In Delvin I became my father,
loved with his love the cherry trees
behind the house where sparrows gathered,
that his dead father's hand implanted;
and the orange seedling the old man teased
into a bush I saw bear fruit
like his own sons moulded in truth
as Catholics, and he a Protestant.

In Delvin I became my father;
walked the darkness to a dead end,
finding no solace in the weather
for the sad thoughts untethered then
of Ballinvalley and old friends
scattered on earth or under it
whose faces time had tampered with
and I would never meet again.

A SCORE OF SPECKLED STARLINGS

Jabbing and crying all the morning long,
a score of speckled starlings on the lawn
glean from the unripe grass Lord knows what
except limp diamonds of last night's frost.

And I would wish them worms in plenty, snails
corpulent and succulent to taste
after their long winter, as well I know
(being a Job's comforter) the hardness of stone.

But all things pass, and these unthinking stare
belie the winter's fragmentary gain,
that joy because a sullen morning brings
sunlight on uncomplicated wings.

EVENING

Over our heads in twos and threes,
convoyed for company, the wild geese
unmelodiously announce
their coming by Castlemaine and once
over the Sliabh Mis mountains bear
towards Kerry Head to winter there –
gannet and goose by God's will
to breed inseparable still.

After them the star-deep sky
darkens and Fenit's blinking eye
surveys with sentinel unease
the black, immeasurable seas.

ISLANDS

Indigenous silence
isolates the islands
as night falls suddenly, taut
like velvet cloth
punctured only in places
where starlight traces
the white line of the sea
in the vicinity.

Denuded but content
they rest from elements
that have driven
men to their graves, given
back to the sea
the half-broken hereditary
land hallowed because
of "Fiche Blian ag Fas."

In summer boats
come and go with goats
and sheep for dispersal,
with an odd interested person
keen to imagine
life as it was in the kitchen
(pure Synge) – hard and bitter
with curraghs adrift in the weather.

The islandman is no more.
By the holy well of Fore
you can meet him, his cap
at a farmer's angle, perhaps
at ease on the rich soil and
pasture, but his mind on the island
knowing again the disease
of damned Atlantic seas.

THE BLACKSMITH

Compelled by circumstance to turn
to welding in an effort to earn
a wage when one time he could choose
the horses to affix with shoes.

He still remembers days that were
heavy with labour and animal stir,
dawn to dusk when a blacksmith stood
more than a cypher in the neighbourhood . . . .

Stung in the sooty atmosphere
of forge, the mounting flames, the queer
shaped colours, he could tell the dark
by the luminosity of a spark;

while tied to the grunting silence horse
stood still, forelegs angled, morse-
tapped until the glittering steel-
clad hoof dropped with a polished peal . . . .

Now days are longer being unfulfilled,
the traffic tone of the horse is stilled
and his image dwindled like the forge's fire –
dying, but yet unwilling to expire.

AUTUMN

Suddenly the air is crisp;
the slightest hardening of stars
contracts the sky; a wisp
of cloud is all that mars
the delicate blue of height
sustained like the sure sky
of Dürer for the night
of incarnation. A cry
of plover overhead,
marked still by the same
note of impending dread –
desolate, tame –
incises expertly
the silence. A scent of musk,
incense of apple tree,
perfume the glowering dusk
with that nostalgic sense
of loss none can reap
from that first inference,
inexplicably deep.

TOO MANY MEMORIES

Can we enter this house now
without sensing your presence there
as we last saw you – dying?
Your room had the damp smell of death –
a musty inertia – a bed on which you were lying

sea-grey and drawn; a print
of Gaugin which you prized and hung
where your eyes could behold it;
a window on silence, which was the world
outside, quiet as a mouse in the cold light.

Too many memories choke the new day.
Can we enter this house now
without the expectancy that the same
sense of sadness shall prevail?
Inevitably someone will draw down your name.

That print of Gaugin I know
you willed to the house, shall it hang
in the room where we last saw you dying?
Expect us when we come, as we shall
some day soon, when memories are not so allying.

THE ISLANDMAN

Cradled on the eastern side
the village – if six houses could be called
a village – to avoid
the fury of the open sea; walled-
in, low slung houses shone
brightly distempered, turf ricks
and cowsheds nearby – a lone
settlement on the island the sea licks
salt, Atlantic storms bruise.

Some will remember the ride
by curragh from the mainland – a cruise
with the turn of the tide
and the waves quiet; and some
will remember the noise-packed, wind-racked run
when the storm came home
first and the sea fouled with a dying sun –
the canvas craft shot like a feather then
on the mountainous back of the sea . . . .

But they were the days of men
who were not afraid – and they fathered me.

SWEN
(as in a glass darkly)

A lone sailor crosses the Atlantic
in an open boat, surviving
hardship, loneliness and the antics
of the elements, to go on living.

An avalanche in Northern Italy
buries a mountain village,
suffocating the inhabitants pitilessly.
In the Baltic an oil spillage

destroys the coastline of Denmark –
marine life, bird life, beaches –
the tanker, listing, bulwark
holed in the collision, reaches

safety, its sea-victim sinks with
a loss of lives. This is "swen".
A Turkish terrorist links with
international anarchic assassins

and guns down the Pope in the Vatican.
The American 6th Fleet on manoeuvres
in disputed waters of the Mediterranean
is annoyed by Libyan jets and over-

reacts. The roving eye of cameras,
the staccato drill of typewriters,
sees all, says all – from Buenos Aires
to Tokyo, Associated Press, Reuters,

copy, enlighten the world with flashes
of daily disasters (including
our own). Nothing escapes the masses,
topics eternally intruding

morning, noon and night, glaring,
overbearing, in the city and beyond,
interrupting with transparent
eloquence lest the public abscond;

as if the oracle had spoken,
as if the image could deceive –
read all about it in your local
paper, watch it on your own T.V.'s!

IN MAY

Outside the window now a blue-tit swings
like an acrobat on a cherry tree,
deep red with blossom, and sings
his pizzicato melody
happy as an itinerant
May-day setting out
on roads inviting and extravagant;
then turning somersaults he cocks a snoot
at me here impotently whorled
within a periwinkle world.

THE HORNED OWL

In the neon light
of the moon the horned owl's
huge eyes become bright
as aureoles.

There is not a star
so penetrating in the skies
as those binocular-
sharp eyes.

Outwardly still
as a huddle of boughs
that are petrified until
a field mouse

ventures some feet
of unsuspecting space
too far to retreat,
but turn about to face

the shock of surreal
wings, the lightning, hair-
splitting steel,
the implacable stare.

CONNEMARA MAN

Over a stony soil his gaunt frame
like an eagle's shadow broods,
furrowed by wind and sea, by labour
no Connemara man eludes.

A sense of water always, a chain-
letter of streams, gaily insistent,
seeking a bed like a tinker man –
gregarious, clacking like a piston

in the silent air. Good man, you stand
astride your nobbled world and wait
the inevitable calm of evening,
as a shepherd dog at the gate,

for the familiar step of God –
a sound that will carry down
to the seashore and over mountain peaks.
A fisherman, you would have known

his feet like a seagull's webbing
the water, predatory deep
at all hours and not be afraid
Stone walls and stony outcrops keep

your dominion worlds away from greed.
Who cannot digest rock or grub from sand
has no part here and would not rise
wrinkled and old above this arid land.

ON THE 25th DAY OF MARCH

A girl in her middle teens dreamt in the quiet
of her sparsely furnished room, a damask cloth
over the open window disarming the light
of an uncompromising sun in its noon onslaught.

In the heat and semi-darkness of the room
did she imagine the angel at her side
closely conversing in the disquieting gloom
of God's design, deferring to her as bride

of the Holy Ghost and mother of His son?
What was she to think or do? She seemed to hear
herself assent, as in a dream. Alone
once more, she trembled with awakening fear

of some unseen intruder in that room,
and felt a spasm of misgiving in her womb.

IN CANDLE-GLOW
OF CHESTNUT

In candle-glow of chestnut
when that tree is blown
with its spring muslin,
when water is brown
with first flood and salmon
and the sky is lark-
high with domed beauty
and light, I mark
the beginning of order
in the things of God,
outward visible signs
of that mystic code;
dreaming in the quiet
how this world was once
the pith of Eden
for Adam and his sons.

IN THE SLOW SUN

The hardening has begun: like frost
that surreptitiously stiffens,
solidifying moisture:
the depth of ice is the degree of cold.

Age has tempered the blood;
a cataclysmic change
occurs – this is the iceman that cometh:
the dispensation of the old.

Mother and father plod in the slow sun;
there is a beauty in frost,
a certain strength in ice,
a usefulness even in mould.

UNDER MOUNT BRANDON

1

Rest now and dream
by the lonely fringe of the Atlantic.
Let the silence redeem
the spent cartridge of mind, frantic
with terror at the thought
of our beloved land torn and destroyed
by intolerance, injustice, rot.

Let us walk side by side
where the gentle waters detonate
on sand rich as gold
that does not encourage hate.
The mountains are old
as Methusaleh, the men,
staunch as the rock that endures,
work wonders with word and pen.

Under Mount Brandon the flowers
of the fuchsia bleed;
the strand is deserted and God-like and free
the grandeur of distance we need
envelops, unites us where we
have watched in the clamouring sack
of our days the children grow strong
as islands out on the sea's back
where islandmen belong.

2

The silence of holy men
breathes in the placid air.
A boat, small as a wren
in the distance moves there
where the waters of the world begin,
on the dark eroded side
of the Blaskets. In Dunquin
there is no room for pride:
a man measures his size
by the ocean, his mind
by the sky – infinite, wise –
and the weight of his words by the wind.

Walking again the quiet strand
at Deelis when the tide is out,
lovers as always, hand-in-hand,
with only a child's exultant shout
to wake the stillness where our own
plunder rock-pools for what they can;
mountains behind us, the unknown
beyond the headland where that man,
Brendan, succumbed (and like him, we,
moved by an inward sense of peace,
of love and love's complicity)
to the strange music of the seas.

FIRST LIGHT

He was born within sight of water;
not a seaman but one who has seen
first light on Derravarragh
when the ghostly reeds gleam
like quicksilver and the grey sky
launches those shafts of returning
light on a quiet world
waking to the music of morning.

Music that never dies –
for born within sight of water
its rhythmic murmur finds
a quiet echo in my father,
gentle yet strong, whose ageing
knows no regrets, no links
weakened by indecision,
only the peace it brings.

ROAD TO THE WEST

The road to the west is afire with fuchsia,
come and see for yourself how each blood-red tree
erupts into flame in the distance and you shall
dance like a firebird there with me.

On to the sky road – Gleann na nGealt –
over the mountains shiny and wet
to Dingle town where the air is salt
with a fisherman's hope for a laden net.

Oh! to be there when a long day closes,
the low sun red as a tallow lamp,
where the fuchsia burns like the bush of Moses –
on the Dingle road to the west of Camp.

IN SUMMER WHEN THE TREES

In summer when the trees
arch with ease
into the egg-shell-blue
wedge of sky,
thoughts are uplifted, too,
correspondingly.

Seldom do we note
the season bloat
with bearing – hidden signs
as fraying edge
of leaf along the lines
of tree and hedge.

And only when the night
falls early, light
stars of coral climb
a painter's sky
we know that summertime
is passing by.

Must all roses die
and you and I
accumulate the dust
of dreams? This is
the blight, the abstract rust
to ruin our kisses.

ON ST. PATRICK'S DAY

We mark the spring beginning
with daffodils that bloom
in March and a cock-bird singing
like a morning-suited groom
on a spikey elderberry
in the garden soon to know
the green and gold of Kerry
after the winter's snow.

We mark the spring beginning
on St. Patrick's Day,
the old men proudly pinning
shamrocks, dew-fresh from the clay;
when to be Irish is all that matters,
and the upsurge in the heart
can mend a mind in tatters
with age-old Irish art.

HER LETTER

Her letter is a tapestry
that tells of changing events
at home, fills in the history
with personal and appropriate comments:

how my father jettisoned rote
to retire at sixty-five,
confident as Don Quixote
in his capacity to survive

unaccustomed tracts of time
and the windmills of boredom: I know
his strength, remember his prime,
support his purposeful show

of aggression and wish him well.
Colourful incidents thread
the words together, tell
of births and deaths and shed

much light on the commentator,
until her beloved face
materialises moments later
in my mind with infinite grace.

The love that binds us together
enriches each paragraph
of her most welcome letter
with quintessence of the distaff.

THE RAINDROP

I cupped my hand to hold the drop of water –
within a world, a world
of atoms and of energy
as concrete and as whorled
as any. When it fell
the distance of some generations
from rosebush thorn
through stem and curled leaf stations
to sting my hand (a craggy space
that time had hacked and worn)
what ages and creations
were halted or still-born?

SOLILOQUY

Trees have only two states,
naked and leafed –
I have a couple of slates
off, a mind reefed
and a soul tortured to death.
Give me room
to draw breath
in this (of our own making) tomb.

Thinking of Fra Angelico
in the light of a colour scheme
or of Michelangelo
seeking to redeem
the lost paradise created for us
by a stroke of his masterly hand –
Adam, lone and audacious,
unloosed on a lotus land.

Nothing approaches death!
if I cry to Eve:
why did you let
Satan achieve
his ambition to force
God into compromise
and us into remorse:
who replies?

Or to Adam if I say:
had you no more
intelligence than we have today,
to partake of sour
fruit in a heavenly place,
meriting for us thereby
the toil, the disgrace:
who will reply?

Who will reply? The whole
earth will cry out in pain,
and the hidden light of the soul
glimmer and darken again
like a candle snuffed out by the wind.
There is no compensation in age
when each day serves to remind
us of our heritage.

If I have a slate off
it is because
the heart and the cloven hoof
obey no laws,
and I am still under
the influence of mammon youth,
oblivious to the dull thunder
of disconcerting truth.

I move with the times,
study the migration of birds,
compose bitter rhymes
by shaping unsuitable words
into a mould
that I like to assert is my own –
and I grow old
under the skin and the bone.

FROST AND SNOW

Snow squads occupy the hills;
they are many and white;
a crystal compactness stills
everything in sight.

Stars squirm in the skies;
the trees are starched with frost;
I see a thrush prise
ice for a discarded crust.

Frost and snow are death;
the same cold applies –
forgetfulness, absence of breath,
and the stone-glass eyes.

DERRYMORE

God's gracious hand
touches the rock; a blaze
of light rainbows the land.
I am Aaron in the days
of Canaan; on every side
a golden aura shields
the thunderous tide;
the up-and-coming fields
rage in their own renewal,
an infectious wind
rippling the pliant pool
of meadow-grass. I find
water in every course,
speckled and brown as trout
and redolent of gorse
when the oblatory fire is out.

MORE PERMANENT THAN CLAY

Sheep were important to him:
the mountains fed them unless the winters
were cold enough for snow,
which was seldom. His home
was dwarfed in its shadow – it loomed
large at dusk and the pigeons
settled early in the wooded slopes.
Day was advanced when the sun zoomed
in on the valley. From the peak
he could see the Atlantic shimmer
like gun-metal and the island sprawl
in white frosting like a cake.
He often dreamed of setting out
like his brothers before him for the States,
returning on holidays with abundance,
and grew sad at the thought.

When his father died he would have sold
out but his mother vacillated;
accustomed to her place at the hearth
she complained of being too old
to settle elsewhere. He stayed –
and as the mountain appeared to increase
he seemed to shrink in its shadow
by comparison. He grew afraid
when his mother died . . . The neighbours came
to sympathise, hinted at marriage
and the blessings of children;
each had a suitable name
to suggest. He drank to excess that night
in an effort to overcome
the feeling of insecurity
that shuddered within him like a sheep with fright.

He stayed – and grew old – alone –
missing his mother's careful hand
in the house (which he neglected,
even failing to limewash the stone).
The sheep were important – they
and the dogs were his confidants –
he could speak to them and be understood.
The mountain stood in his way
like a monstrous tombstone God had made
more permanent than clay.

THE FISHERMAN

Only the murmur of water on stones,
the long hook of the sun scything
the shadows. He is at one with the silence,

remote on the river bank, his line
trailing in the current that takes the rod
in tow, divining the shallows.

Does he dream between catches? What thoughts
spring from inaction, while the world whirls
on its axis, shaping the future

through aeons of patient attention? Father,
in me and in ours advances
the evolution of thought, caught

like the trout in moments of deep pleasure
to the sound of water honing the senses
in a fine awareness.

SPAILPIN

We are far from the hills
of our beginnings – the sun
seems to rise in the wrong place
as if the world itself was spun.

If their accents jar on us,
how much stranger ours to them –
the soft brogue of the west,
ballast of mountainy men?

At night when the work is done,
the pipes drawing and free,
we stay together and talk
of our hills by the sea.

They say one place is as good
as the next, that life is the same
in county Leitrim as Kerry,
but there's more to it than a name.

Even the air is different,
the wind has a crueller bite,
and we know on a given morning
the feel of the land's not right.

Thank God the days are numbered
by the cross fields we till
on our way back to Tubrid
and our beloved hills.

MESPIL ROAD

Water discovered the lock
like a level lost and found:
I pictured Patrick Kavanagh
lamenting the hills that surround

Rocksavage – thoughts, words,
slipping in and out of mind
like eels in water-reeded gloom –
a sense of hopelessness combined

with apathy, memory like a salmon
spent on that inland course
where souls shudder to an end –
even his own old horse

given wings and a free rein,
mentally grounded again.

THE SNAIL

It lugs the damaged shell
like a ruin about its head.

Imagine the panic suffused
in that silvery thread

of progress, the pumping
of valve and piston, the torc

of body and tail,
the twin horns like a fork

prodding, the head low
as a horse in a field

ploughing, intent on a hazy
horizon to rebuild

its defences under cover
of grass, from the tiptoe

dance of the demon thrush,
the gait of the crow.

A MARRIAGE IN HEAVEN

We rise with the wisdom of another day:
in that time others have learned to die

without regret. Some see it as age
but there is more to it than approaching the edge

of the absolute. There are moments to relive
together, faded photographs of love

that show us like offspring of ourselves,
unbelievably young – a progression that involves

children, change, a telescoping of time
to eternal ticks – a universal theme.

It has no end – did it ever have an end?
Together we have seen our love expand,

have become one in the impossible manner of God,
no less individual, unanimously good.

REWARD
(for Donal Murphy)

The plimsolled sun with its salmon markings
eases into the water in the far west,
beyond known and fabled islands, darkening
the bruised sky as night ships in

on schedule, with a comfortable suggestion
                              of sleep
for seasoned lobster men. The sea
rocks with a lullaby lilt on the step
of the slip and curraghs quartered there

collide with each other. Life is the sum
of turmoil, an encounter with the elements,
                              day
the extent of light, winter or summer,
with little to show but a shoreside yard

and a house, the third of a boat – not like
                             writing
a poem where the labour is its own reward.

AUTUMN HORIZON

1

Light the lamp, draw the curtain now,
the leaves have fallen.
In the quiet I hear them curl

against the door, and should I open it
they would fall in,
dying like spent salmon, corroded, the green

pigment a patchwork of copper and old gold
dried to a parchment –
the landmark of chestnut and beech and oak.

2

Not all the care of a computer
can halt the march, end
the decidual rite of time,

the clockwork precision of God, the beauty
that grinds to a bitter
dust in due season. O let them ride

in their last abandon the roads of a rusting world –
they will not litter
long the grey façade that is our horizon.

WIZARDRY

I remember my father building a shed
to store timber and turf in in the days
before the war – sawing, planing, he'd
manage something out of nothing always.

He had a way with him and could turn
his hand to any task – an alchemist
with base materials – could worm
fish out of water, which he did to exist

in difficult times. I never had his flair
for extemporising nor his skill
with the hands – except for pen and paper,
juxtaposing words out of a still

of mental fermentation, which
some marvelled at and others dismissed
as inconsequential gibberish.
But words outlast the very best

of workmanship in wood or stone
to find a permanence in memory;
and so I set these symbols down
in recognition of his wizardry.

ROOTS

If I had a four-acre field
with nothing but grass
and wind-knitted hedges
to encompass it,

with rose-hip and blackberry
bruises, sloe-
blue and elder and haw,
I would never know

This hunger of heart
that every now and again
surfaces with a pang
of unaccountable pain –

a hereditary tremor
waking within
like the sense of loss accrued
from original sin.

But with a four-acre field
tenanted without words
by meek, indigenous creatures
and indigent birds,

I would walk the perimeter
feeling absurdly proud,
my feet light on the grass,
my head in the clouds.

SEASCAPE, FENIT

The high wind excites the sea;
waves like white mice dash
and disappear; there are three
steps visible to the pier

with small boats buoyed and riding
the swell, darkness coming in
with rain over Brandon, hiding
its head in the distance. The bright speck

of a seagull is now the source of light,
the beginning of awareness. I let
my mind collapse and the sight
eke from my eyes to slowly dissolve

as an aspirin in water, my spirit
waking to the sensation like a tiny bivalve.

EVENING

The boats harden against the tide,
become locked in reflections, bulging, contracting,
in a blood-bath that is the sea
on the final phase of a summer evening.
Gulls that have followed them home are annoyed
that there is no waste, circle and wheel
into the path of the sun, their dark
shadows staining the water like tea,
and the silence stoned by their raucous screaming.

By now the boats have nosed the cold
sea-weeded pier, have been bound to rings
in the eternal pattern of all creation,
while men, morose as they disembark
empty-handed, give vent to bitter words.

The moon rises beyond the skyline
dappling with light the continuous scene,
and like an old fossil that nobody heeds
a grey owl hoots and airs his wings.

GOD GAVE THEM THE MOUNTAINS FOR SHEEP

God gave them the mountains for sheep –
where else could they graze
when good land is not cheap
and poor men struggle to survive?

They are two hardy breeds
on a low level of sustenance;
one follows where the other leads:
there is no envy in their lives.

Sure-footed at staggering heights,
they would climb Mount Olympus
to trouble the gods for their rights
to the grass, yet survey

acres of pastureland green as can be
and seldom be tempted to stray.

THE YEAR IS BEGUN

The year is begun:
the first tendrils sparkle in the sun.
Above me in dark-threaded trees
three pigeons settle ill-at-ease;
on a roof-top a thrush calls
fearfully at sound of my footfalls.
I feel exalted on the rim
of the universe, united with Him
in a flow of life that must be
immeasurable in immensity.

Last night we spoke of God and man;
you, with explicit trust, began
recounting ways by which you came
to the counting-house of His name.
We quoted Kung, Teilhard and others –
Aquinas, Augustine, the fathers
and Apostles – going back to genesis
and beyond – the fearful abyss
where no light penetrates or finds
a way for uncertain minds.

I was Thomas, the doubting one,
dissatisfied as to how it begun,
sceptical as to why
archangels should fall from on high –
if heaven were what we were taught
how could its inhabitants be not
happy or content,
knowing God to the full extent?
how could they pride themselves above
the source of love?

We spoke of species, tried to explain
how primates could never attain
the intelligence of man; how no
crossed species could sow
seed and root
anything better than brute.
In the end I had to admit
without faith to sustain it
theological doubt could destroy
my sanity.

Now I promise to be
full of humility
for the new year; I will take
Christ at his word and forsake
the elements of doubt that explode
like an atom in the face of God . . .
The birds sing –
I feel that I could take wing
(if I but flapped my arms) and fly
like that blackbird scouring the sky.

I HAVE DIED A HUNDRED
NIGHTS' DEATH

I have died a hundred nights' death for you
because I was born with a kink
not to accept life but be murdered by
a doubtful ability to think.

Often I have lain awake with a snow moon
mirrored on white sheets and my face
wet with tears of self pity, my body
drained like an empty pillow case,

and have tried to divine the future, make known
the anguish and sorrow confronting you
breaking my own heart, beating like Don Quixote
dark sails of time until I was blue.

I would have been better employed allowing the
                        body to sleep,
leave time care for you, darlings, as it has
for man since the days of Adam, and be bent
with the winds in the manner of grass.

In the manner of grass grow and be scythed down
to make room for fresh shoots that shall bear
the pain and the love through a new generation
ascending a step further the stair.

THE SWANS AT BLENNERVILLE

1

As long as I remember
each year the swans returned to breed
on this bright water

investing it with beauty.
At dusk I loved to watch them feed
in the white reflection

of their loveliness.

2

One by one the great eggs broke
until in time

six cygnets tumbled in
like quick grey puffs of cannon smoke
shot into line,

follow-the-leader fashion.

3

Thereafter day by day they grew
more confident

of eye and plunging neck,
enlarging body with its hue
of white beginning . . .

4

Sudden as nightfall,
mute, but with a voice of wings,
I saw them lift

into the stunned silence –
sons and daughters of high kings
enrobed with snow.

TURNING FOR HOME

Turning for home, wind in our ears like song,
skies burned down to the horizon's level now,
the first white streaks of land *something is wrong*
tremble before us – *waves pound at the bow,*
the masthead snaps, is flung somewhere behind.
With the sudden fury of storm the sea runs green
and angry *the others rushing about blind*
to secure the boat and rain deluges the scene.

A voice calls in the darkness petering out
in a whine. The boat topples and waves break
over us *the bitter taste of salt in the mouth,*
a hand grasping a spar. A star is awake,
its cold light silvering down the sand
the silent and indomitable land.

SHEILA

Bright as cherry blossom
in her pink pyjamas and (thank God)
not too sick this time, she lords it
like a mandarin over the other
patients in the children's ward,
not yet four, but a veteran sufferer –
independent, resourceful – and to me
as beautiful as cherry blossom
on a May-young tree.

CARILLON

Listen long enough, quietly intent –
above the sea, that sad harmonium
of sound, rising and falling,
is there not a tintinnabulum
of bells, like sea shells pounded
by tides, ground to perfection, a ring
of wind can toll in the ageless silence?

Time is a benediction: a bent
monk in grey distinction, calling
with famished hand, the sailors back
from the wanton sea, his pale face aghast . . .

A lengendary file of fathers, winding the steep track
half-way to heaven; or composite in cells,
age like an ass's cross on each,
light as a blade of grass,
hearing the bells tinkle and the cry of birds
in sanctuary, the end-dream of detachment,
the culmination of words.

Above the sea when the sun suffuses Leary's Island
with liquid light and the white spume
dwindles into dark, I hear the bells'
eternal summons in the gloom.

A PRAYER IN WINTER

Thank you, Lord, too, for the cold
that reminds me of you whom I might
otherwise be disposed to forget
if the day were right. The white

menace, snow, slicks suddenly
on the hills, figures in wind and sky
like a bad dream I wake up to.
Francis De Sales used say we

could never appreciate spring
without winter to measure it by . . .
Your winter, Lord,
is the indifference I employ

to obstruct your love on a day
when it might seem unnecessary to pray.

RAIN

The rain had that certain
indefinable note of nostalgia
that released memories from inertia . . .
I thought of groping roads

near Mullingar, bright with
ablution, and fields floating
in mist; of windscreen wipers
itching at the glass and tyres

of the little Ford dividing
the water that streamed on macadam
like a black sea; of the hidden
house that only my father

knew, somewhere in the grey
distance, vague and unfathomable.

MASTERPIECE

Genius begets genius. Consider
Cervantes' Don Quixote, madder
than the Mad Hatter, anachronistic knight
whose dream of chivalry upset
La Mancha, whose imaginative vision
mocked the world. A fatal inquisition
doomed his rage and folly.
Faithful Sancho Panza followed
his knight on the merry-go-round
of madness, though severely in the background –
a presence one senses rather
than perceives – is anything sadder?

Yes. The blotch in Daumier's picture
depicting the squire and the caricature
of the lank, featureless Don with his gear
on a grey, emaciated mare,
slight as an arrow struck
(like the slender hand of a clock
that is poised forever) in that absurd pose
the artist conjured out of prose.

THE MAGIC OF CARAGH
(for Mary)

Was the lake water blue
the quality of abstract skies,
or was it the colour
of your dreaming eyes
I remember, the dreams dreamt
by the young and not so wise?

Rhododendrons flowered
in lilac and magenta; these
I remember – the olive-dark leaves
luminous like wax trees –
and our talk of marriage, children
and responsibilities.

If the young were wise
the world would be always old,
and nothing could ever happen
that was not foretold
or expected, and beauty lessened
and love lost to the bold.

Lovelier than the memory,
now we are old and wise,
is the love biding
in your bluer-than-lake-blue-eyes –
all that was ever beautiful to me,
beautiful and wise.

CATCHING THE LIGHT

Where we stood the bogland dried
to a brown crust, like bread baked
in a griddle. The mountains died
in the distance, propped up

against the sky like a mound
or neolithic burial place.
The Smearla flashed by drowned
rocks and drenched vegetation,

catching the light like a mirror.
Generations apart, our lines
straked the belly of the river.

Water and the elusive trout
found an outlet in the sea.

Age, inevitably, found us out.

BASIN ROAD BLUES

An ugly wire fence surrounds it,
infilled and levelled to hold
giant reels of cable and machinery.
I remember it of old

when the tidal waters flushed it,
scouring the soft grey silt
that built from neglect – amorphous mud
bulging like a stitched quilt –

and the stiff crane that rusted away
to a memory. I learned to swim there
by the slip, its commercial importance
having gone by then with the care-

taker of the locks, left unemployed,
and the great gates gagged for the tide.

IT WAS MAY DAY
BEFORE SHE SET OUT

It was May day before she set out
on the long journey through the hills;
already the road was a dustpan with drought
and the sun a dazzling attendant.

She looked forward to seeing Elizabeth
again; they had always been close,
particularly so since her mother's death:
Elizabeth would be pleased with her news.

Would she believe her? She felt she would:
she needed to get away from the house
and the hurt, the knowing look and nod
of the neighbours, poor Joseph's disbelief.

The road stretched right across Judea –
it was a long road that had no relief.

97

ANTHONY, PARING AN APPLE

Knife-edge to roundness,
the glistening blade
slits the veneer of skin.

Escaping essence clouds
and assails the senses –
juice ripples and runs
the slippery slopes of steel,
lodging in crevices of fingers,
whetting desire with its
orchard-leavened smell.

The knife skims like a plough,
deftly manoeuvering.
Peel, like a paper cut-out,
curls precariously
as the naked flesh is revealed
with the sensuous, consummate
art of the striptease.

RELATIONS

I retain the impression of two
elderly relatives at the door
of an elevated house
waving good-bye as our

Ford car slowly moved off –
a sister and brother, aunt
and uncle to my father,
who farmed a grant

of land in Monaghan –
unmarried, at a remove
from the rest of the family,
with none at hand to love,

grown old and almost forgotten,
wanting one of their own
to inherit the place.
We were accustomed to town,

to running water and drains,
convenient to shops and schools,
complacent civilisation.
My father, though handy with tools,

knew little or nothing of land.
And I can visualise them still
as I saw them then,
on a gentle northern hill,

the once and only time
in life I ever met
this lonely couple I am
reluctant to forget,

who were akin to me –
faces I cannot shape
now death has intervened
to shatter the inscape.

HOME
(for Micheal O'Rourke)

I see it at its best –
breathtakingly beautiful,
the sun divining the sand,
the sea like a jewel
on the marriage finger
of Sliabh Mis (the Maharees) –
bride of excellence
in everything she is.

Even when the clouds
corral the sleeping giant,
Baurtregaum, and shadows, dark
as tongues of defiant
Tuatha De Danann, purple
the slopes, the great ridge
my father twice crossed
spans like a bridge

the gulf between past and present,
time and eternity.
A sphinx, still-born,
with lion paws in the sea,
whose once woods echoed
to cries of philandering men –
Fionn, the Fianna, Cuchulainn –
triggering fancy again.

Camp, Killelton, Derrymore,
Deelis, Aughasla – names
conjured of magic and meaning
from the rust-rich flames
of the fuchsia, connive
with the lotus-lilt of the seas
to detain for the heart's surrender
a less obdurate Ulysses.

From DIMENSIONS

*(a series of poems suggested by incidents
related in Twenty Years a' Growing and
The Islandman)*

7

When the spring tide ebbed
women and children jostled
on the strand gathering limpets
and winkles that clung like fossils

to the rocks. A channel
could be crossed at low water
to Woman's Island and mother
with Joan and her daughter

gathered their skirts together
between their legs to wade
the narrow stream. Unthinking,
they let the incoming tide

cut them off from the strand
as the channel filled to the height
of a man. I was sent
to alert the menfolk who brought

a ladder full twenty feet long
with them with which to straddle
the water – one end locked
in a crevice, the other cradled

in sand and held firm
for the frantic women to cross
carefully so as not to upset
the balance. Nevertheless,

Joan did and fell,
limpets and winkles flying
from her loosened apron, headlong
into the tide, crying

like a snared rabbit or gull
wilfully thrown in the wind
of a storm. Only my father
had the presence of mind

to jump in after her
to bring her safely to land.
The limpets and winkles, however,
were lost to the sand.

9

Onset of sunset, the sea becalmed,
the silence well-water deep,
measured to the creak of oars,
blades dipping rhythmically,
catapulting the curragh to the shore,
lightly, easily, the oarsmen straining,
bending, drawing, their shoulders snared
in gold light like gilt,
their eyes dredging those pin-points of light
from the island, faint as first stars aired
in the drifting dark of the sky
(the seaman's compass) – now within sight,
and the great shelf of the island
looming from the shadows; the welcoming cry
of a petrel transcending the suck
of the water on the prow
as the last quick strokes are struck
and the boat rides to the quiet harbour,
where words are prised from them
like limpets from forgotten rock.

25

Water has tagged me,
like a man toting his past;
the incompatible sea
is my companion to the last.

In the night
the cold down of the tide
seems beside me, light
as the bed gown of a bride.

The ebb and flow
is such that thoughts attune
to the tow
of the magnetic moon.

Rising and going down –
always the same – this sea
that would as easily drown
the islands as me.

28

Away from the islands I dream
of the sea, ebb and flow,
the pitch black curragh abeam
in the current's undertow;
the oarsmen straining, the wind
flicking the waves to foam,
the spent sun behind
and before us our island home.

Often at night I wake
thinking I hear a cry:
a storm about to break,
the islandmen at sea.
Too many homes bereft,
too many memories
for those of us who are left
to forget in times of ease.

O Blasket Islandman,
where can you hide? In what
far continent can
you exorcise the thought
of curraghs racing behind
a mackerel shoal on the run,
or ever erase from the mind
days of growing and done?